INNER GOLD

By the Same Author

Balancing Heaven and Earth: A Memoir
with Jerry M. Ruhl

Contentment: A Way to True Happiness
with Jerry M. Ruhl

Ecstasy: Understanding the Psychology of Joy

Femininity Lost and Regained

He: Understanding Masculine Psychology

Inner Work: Using Dreams and Active Imagination for Personal Growth

Living Your Unlived Life: Coping with Unrealized Dreams and Fulfilling Your Purpose in the Second Half of Life
with Jerry M. Ruhl

Lying with the Heavenly Woman: Understanding and Integrating the Feminine Archetypes in Men's Lives

Owning Your Own Shadow: Understanding the Dark Side of the Psyche

She: Understanding Feminine Psychology

The Fisher King and the Handless Maiden: Understanding the Wounded Feeling Function in Masculine and Feminine Psychology

Transformation: Understanding the Three Levels of Masculine Consciousness

We: Understanding the Psychology of Romantic Love

INNER GOLD

Understanding Psychological Projection

ROBERT A. JOHNSON

koa books

A Division of Chiron Publications
Asheville, North Carolina

Koa Books is a book imprint of Chiron Publications.
www.koabooks.com
www.ChironPublications.com

Edited by Arnold Kotler
Cover design © 2008 by Ayelet Maida, A/M Studios
Text design © 2008 by Brigitte Bolos
Cover art by Louis Pohl, Sea Series No. 8,
used with permission of Louis Pohl Gallery
Printed in the United States of America

ISBN 978-1-63051-463-1 Paperback

Publisher's Cataloging-in-Publication
Johnson, Robert A., 1921–
Inner gold : understanding psychological projection /
Robert A. Johnson. — Kihei, Hawai'i : Koa Books, ©2008. p. ; cm.
ISBN: 978-0-9773338-2-0
1. Projective identification. 2. Projections (Psychology) 3. Self-actualization (Psychology) 4. Spiritual life. I. Title.
BF175.5.P68 J64 2008
155.2/84—dc22 0807
2 3 4 5 6 7 8 9 / 14 13 12 11 10

Contents

CHAPTER ONE

INNER GOLD

CHAPTER ONE

Projecting Your Gold

My first analyst, Fritz Kunkel, said that there are three ways to learn psychology: "Read Greek mythology, read Jung, and watch. Watching is best." I learn so much from watching, and one of the things I observe most carefully is the exchange of inner, alchemical gold. Inner gold is the highest value in the human psyche. It is our soul, the Self, the innermost part of our being. It is us at our best, our twenty-four-karat gift to ourselves. Everyone has inner gold. It isn't created, but it does have to be discovered. When I speak about gold this way, I am also speaking about God. These are two ways to describe the mystery.

When we awaken to a new possibility in our lives, we often see it first in another person. A part of us that has been hidden is about to emerge, but it doesn't go in a straight line from our unconscious to becoming conscious. It travels by way of an intermediary, a host. We project our gold onto someone, and suddenly we're consumed with that person. The first inkling of this is when the other person appears to be so luminous that he (or she) glows in the dark. That's a sure sign that something is changing in us and we are projecting our gold onto the other person.

When we observe the things we attribute to the other person, we see our own depth and meaning. Our gold goes first from us to them. Eventually it will come back to us. Projecting our inner gold offers us the best chance for an advance in consciousness.

The Medieval Mind

In the Middle Ages, the work of alchemy was to produce gold from base metals. There were charlatans trying to make actual gold, but the best alchemists were those working with the gold of the spirit.

Alchemy comes from a time when the medieval mind was at its highest flowering. In medieval times, people did not divide reality into inner and outer or even acknowledge a difference between the two. For them, inside and outside were the same. To accomplish all that we have today, we've had to split the world in two. We couldn't be this competitive with a medieval mind. But the price we pay for our accomplishments is loneliness and an inability to love. When we're in love, we *are* our beloved. I spent many years trying to help people differentiate between inner and outer: You are you, and I am I. Your husband is your husband. We have not yet completed the transition to the modern mind. Many psychological problems are a failure to differentiate between *out there* and *in here.*

According to the teachings of India, the external world is *maya,* illusion. It is considered illusory because it is actually within, not *out there.* We see only the "ten thousand things" that we project. In ancient China, Lao Tzu dreamed of a butterfly, and for the rest of his life he didn't know whether he had dreamed the butterfly or the butterfly had dreamed him.

In the West, gold is the symbol of the Self, while in the East, the symbol of our inner divinity is the diamond. In their interior meanings, they are the same, but the images are different. Diamonds are the hardest matter on earth—unearthly, celestial, and impersonal. Gold is much softer, a matter of relationship, the Self as related. I think we're lucky to have gold to cope with.

The Glow in Your Eyes

When we see that we have given our spiritual gold to someone to hold for us, there are several ways we might respond. We could go to him or her and say, "The meaning of my life has suddenly appeared in the glow in your eyes. May I tell you about it?" This is another way of saying, "I have given you my inner gold. Will you carry it for me for a while?" But we rarely say and do things that directly. Instead, we stand across the room, turn our back on him, and feel totally frightened, stumbling and carrying on in odd ways. We meet at the coffee pot during the morning break at work and banter with each other, speaking all kinds of nonsense. We joke and laugh, and an animated play goes on. Then, when we head back to work, we feel energized and brightened for the day. It was not the coffee. It was the exchange of inner, alchemical gold.

The exchange of gold is a mysterious process. It is *our* gold, but it's too heavy for us, so we need someone else to carry it for a time. That person becomes synonymous with meaning. We follow him with an eagle eye wherever he goes. His smile can raise us to heavenly heights, his frown will hurl us to hellish depths, so great is the power of meaning.

Hero Worship

Sometimes the exchange of gold takes the form of hero worship. For a ten-year-old boy, his twelve-year-old neighbor is a hero. The ten-year-old wants to imitate him. He walks like him. He wears shoes just like his. He borrows his vocabulary and hangs around him as much as he can. We all know the power of fashion, and especially how fashion runs through a neighborhood of adolescents. The style of shoes, prisoner pants, all those things you've got to have. It's both inspiring and funny to watch somebody hero-worship.

Two years later, when the ten-year-old is twelve, he has become the characteristics that he projected onto the twelve-year-old. He assimilated them back and became them. Now he hero-worships a fourteen-year-old and has a new ladder to climb.

I remember vividly my own early hero worshipping. It was so strong. Slowly and painfully, I've drawn those hero-worship projections—this placing of my own potential onto others—back to myself. Turning gray in the process, I have become what I was hero-worshipping.

Hunting for Gold

When I was fourteen, I drove with my grandmother to Spokane, Washington, to attend a family funeral. One of my cousins, a little older than I, had married, and I saw her husband for the first time. Instantly, he became my hero. I was unstable in that period of my life. My feet didn't work well, and I hadn't really entered the masculine world—I'm not greatly endowed in that direction.

His name was Thor. He was of Norwegian ancestry, in his early twenties, a big, strong guy, an absolute master of the physical world. That fellow did something so kind and important for me. The day after the funeral, he plucked me out of the family gathering and took me into the woods to go hunting, the first and last hunting I've ever done. He sensed who I was, what I needed, and at what speed to initiate me. He knew I had to be told which end of the gun to point where, and he did it all so well. He was a God-Man, someone of infinitely high value for me. I was envious and bound to him, almost literally. I placed my feet in his footsteps as we walked through the forest, giddy with his greatness.

Suddenly he stopped and said, "Squirrel on a limb. Over there." Ten or twenty yards away was a squirrel on a pine branch. "All right," he said, and told me exactly what to do: "Line this up with the squirrel. Pull the trigger gently, so you don't jiggle the gun and lose him out of sight. It'll go bang in your ear. Don't be afraid." I did it, and of course I thought I'd missed the squirrel. "Come on," he said, and we went over. And lo and behold, I hadn't missed. There on the ground under the limb was a ragged, bloody mess of a squirrel. I was so proud and so horrified at the same time. I learned in a split second what heroism costs you and what it gives you. I had become a big man, but I couldn't stand it. I did not want to shoot squirrels. We went back home, and I was more pleased than unhappy.

Giving Back

Forty years later, I got a letter from my cousin, Thor's wife: "You must be Bob. My granddaughter brought a book home from her psychology class by Robert Johnson, and I think it must be you." I hadn't seen or heard from her in more than forty years. We spoke on the phone, and she asked if she could visit for her sixtieth birthday.

What a wonderful time we had! She brought a small entourage of people, among whom was a young

Thor, the grandson of my hero. He was the same age I had been when I knew the first Thor. And he was skinny and frightened, the way I'd been, quickly going down in the whirlpool of the modern world. My head was swimming with possibilities. So I entertained young Thor with the story of my first and only hunting trip, talking about his grandfather and the wonderful day he had given me. Unfortunately, the elder Thor had drunk himself to death and was pretty much a failure in his life. My cousin had divorced him, and he just went down skid row. I didn't like hearing this. He had been my hero.

So I told this little guy, who hadn't said a word, "I owe your grandfather an immense debt, and I transfer that debt to you. I owe you whatever you need from me." The boy latched on to me immediately, and I became his hero. It was a beautiful exchange.

This is alchemical gold. You put your own gold onto somebody until you're able to hold it yourself. As a fourteen-year-old, I couldn't do what Thor could. He was twenty-four or twenty-five, and I put my gold onto him, the gold of masculinity, strength, courage, and independence, things I had none of and he had lots.

Over the course of forty years, I got my gold back. I didn't do it by way of guns—I've never shot a gun since. I was acutely aware of all this as I sat next to young Thor. "I have gold for you," I said. Of course, it was his gold, or it wouldn't work. I couldn't give him anything. But I could carry his gold, if he chose to allow me. And he did, because I'm more like him and he's more like me than either of us is like his grandfather.

I've made my way in this world by a series of carriers of specific gold. With the aid of heroes, I've proceeded in the way an alpine climber hammers in his piton, secures his rope, pulls himself up to the piton, and gets hold of it. This is how we grow. Everyone comes to be where he or she is now, to some extent, through the exchange of gold.

Sometimes We Have to Struggle

When the exchange of gold proceeds well, we mature and eventually become strong enough to ask for our gold back. It might be awkward at first. We might have to slam the door as we exit, to convince ourselves that we're leaving. We act in this kind of adolescent way, clumsy at retrieving our gold, because we don't really understand what's going on.

Carrying someone's gold is a fine art and a high responsibility. If you are the recipient of someone's gold, hold it carefully and be prepared to give it back within a microsecond's notice. Unfortunately, there are people who collect gold and refuse to give it back. It's a kind of murder. They collect an entourage or followers and exploit them. It happened to me, and it was exceedingly painful.

My father didn't really father me, and so much of the fatherly gold in me was uninvested. I spent a good part of my early life looking for the father I never had. One day when I was in my twenties, a man came into my life who seemed ideal for this investment of gold. He acted like a father and let it be known that he would carry the masculine archetype for me. I trusted him and was ready for a wise, old man to guide me to the next stage of life. Here was someone in whose glory I could bask. I gave him my gold, and it was a wonderful experience—for a few days.

Within a week, he began manipulating and dominating me, organizing my life and using me. I could have stayed, and that would have been the price for storing my fatherly gold with him. But I already knew too much to allow him to keep it. So I asked for my gold back. He wouldn't return it. He wanted to continue the manipulation. I had to fight with him, not with blows, but psychologically. I fought my way out of his orbit, and there is still enmity between us. It was a bitter experience.

Our culture understands little about these matters, so when we ask the other person for our gold back, she probably won't know what we're talking about. She might say, "Last week you were opening doors for me and treating me like a princess, and this week you're ignoring me." People don't understand the dynamics. It is only *after* you get your gold back that you can see the gold of the other person. When the time is right, when you are ready to bear the weight, you must get your gold back. If you can do it with dignity and tact, that's best. But you must get it back, one way or another.

Creating a Ceremony

It is possible to create a ceremony to mark the important occasion of returning someone's gold. A young man I was seeing in analysis gave me a large chunk of his gold. From the beginning, he'd compliment me every time we saw each other. I'd say, "This is your value. You need to drape it around my neck for a while, but you're going to take it back eventually," using this language. He kept complimenting me, telling me how valuable I was to him, how lucky he was to have me as his therapist. "You're talking about your own inner gold," I told him.

He was an intelligent and powerful young man, a genius in his own right, and his gold was too heavy for him. He was desperate for someone to take it off his shoulders. So we discussed what was happening and the terms of the exchange, and he fully understood. This went on for almost five years. Then, one day, he said, "I want my gold back." I had noticed that he was getting restless, so I agreed. "Things are changing," I said. "Let's do a ceremony to put the gold back in your pocket."

I conjured up a small piece of gold, the size of a pea, and a few days later we had the ceremony. He held the kernel of gold, shaking, suddenly more aware of what he had been doing. Then he put it in my hands and said, anxiously, "Suppose you don't give it back?"

I said, "Yeah, suppose." I kept the gold for a while, held it in my hand, put it in my pocket, waited a bit, and produced it again. Then I ceremoniously put it back into his hands, and he was greatly relieved. I said, "This is your gold, and it belongs only in your pocket. I am honored that you would allow me to hold it for you all these years. But it's yours, and now it needs to go back to you." It was a profound moment, a coming-of-age. I had paved the way for returning it when the time was right. Being clear about what is taking place and what is the desired outcome can be very helpful.

It didn't actually go this easily. The next day, he had his gold all over me again. He couldn't hold it and wanted me to take it back. The exchange of gold is not entirely a voluntary matter. Sometimes it takes a few round trips. We traded the gold back and forth several more times until one day he could withstand it. Since then, I haven't heard any more about him wanting it back.

Don't Mix Levels

When gold is being exchanged, there are two rules that can save both parties trouble. First, when you put your gold onto someone, you have no right to pester that person. To project meaning and importance onto another person is enough. You don't want to smother him. Second, don't mix levels. Alchemical gold is an element in its own right and shouldn't be mixed with anything else. Friendship, companionship, sex, fun, work—all these relationships can be good, but it creates a mess when you express the alchemical gold through them. You may end up marrying the person who carries your gold. That's legitimate. But don't mix the gold with the many other facets of relationship that are possible. "Blessed are the pure in heart." Pure means unmixed. On what level is it true? On what level is the Virgin birth true?

Almost all psychological suffering is caused by mixing levels. Everything in you is good in its own right, a construct of God. But contamination of one thing by another can short-circuit both. Much of my time as a therapist was spent making an effort to get patients to state as simply as possible the elements of their problem. As soon as the issues are understood clearly, it's usually clear what to do.

When you are struck, when gold is being exchanged, sit quietly until the smoke clears and you see where you are. If you can talk this out with the person holding your gold—with all the dignity and intelligence you can muster—it's a beautiful way of affirming what is going on. It may be risky, but it is well worth the effort.

Love and Marriage

Sometimes, when you put your gold onto another person, he also puts his gold onto you. It gets complicated when the exchange of gold goes both ways. One of the contaminations of levels that we make—

we're scarcely able to think otherwise—is that the exchange of gold means marriage. Marriage is good, and gold is good. They may go together nicely. But they're not synonymous. It can be a problem when we mix these things up. We think, I've fallen in love, I must take her to bed. Maybe you will, but that's not synonymous with falling in love.

In our culture, mutual projection is regarded as the prerequisite for marriage. We take for granted that we will marry the person we are *in love* with. But being in love is not enough to guarantee a successful marriage. When you fall in love, you feel overwhelmed with excitement. You've projected your gold, your deepest inner value, onto the other person. You've given it to her to incubate for a while, until you are ready to take it back. And if the feeling is mutual, she has given her gold to you.

For the relationship to succeed, somewhere along the way each of you has to take your gold back. Unfortunately, that's usually accompanied by disillusionment. "You're not the knight I thought you were." "You're not a princess when you wake up in the morning." The gold comes clattering down by way of disappointment. If we could only understand that we put our gold in someone's lap for a period of time—until we get stronger—and someday it will come to an end. We aren't wise in this respect, and it's one of the most painful issues in our culture. Five years later, when the relationship isn't working, we don't understand that it's time for us to withdraw our projection and actually relate to the other person —our partner, our spouse.

True marriage can only be based on human love, which is different from romantic love, being in love, or in-loveness. Romanticism is unique to the West, and is a relatively new occurrence, only since the twelfth century. Romantic love is not a basis for marriage. Our human life, our marriage, is fed by the capacity to love human to human. When we're in love, we put our gold—our expectations—on the other person, and this obliterates her. There is no relatedness.

Loving is a human faculty. We love someone for who that person is. We appreciate and feel a kinship and a closeness. Romantic love, on the other hand, is a kind of divine love. We deify the other person. We ask that person, without knowing it, to be the incarnation of God for us. Being *in love* is a deep religious experience, for many people the only religious experience they'll ever have, the last chance God has to catch them.

Gold Is Close to God

One reason we hesitate to carry our own gold is that it is dangerously close to God. Our gold has Godlike characteristics, and it is difficult to bear the weight of it.

In Indian culture, there's a time-honored custom that you have the right to go to another person—a man, a woman, a stranger—and ask him or her to be the incarnation of God for you. There are strict laws governing this. If the person agrees to be the incarnation of God for you, you must never pester him. You must never put a heavy weight on him—it's weighty enough as it is. And you must not engage in any other kind of relationship with that person. You don't become friends, and you don't marry him. The person becomes a kind of patron saint for you.

J. Krishnamurti was a wonderful man. Lots of people put gold on him. One afternoon, he and I went for a walk in Ojai, California, and a little old lady was kneeling alongside the path. We just walked by. Later he told me, "She has put the image of God on me. She knows what she's doing. She never talks or asks anything of me. But when I go for a walk, she somehow knows where I'm going to be, and she's always there." What was most touching was his attitude. If she needed this, he would do it.

This is the original meaning of the terms *godfather* and *godmother*. That person is the carrier of Godlike qualities for you. Nowadays we think of a godparent as the one who will take care of us materially in case our parents are not able to see it through. But the original meaning was of someone who carries the subtle part of your life—a parent in an interior, Godlike way. It's a wonderful custom. Most parents are worn out just seeing their child through to physical maturity. We need someone else who isn't bothered with authority issues, like "How much is my allowance this week?" Being a godparent was originally a quiet arrangement for holding a child's gold.

When I was sixteen, two years after meeting Thor, I desperately needed someone like that. So I appointed a godmother and godfather, and those two people saved my life. They knew instinctively the duties of this need, and they fulfilled them. My godmother died when I was twenty-two, and I wasn't ready to give her up. It was the most difficult loss of my life. I was forced to take my gold back before I was ready. My godfather lived until I was in my fifties, and by then I was ready to let him go.

I love the idea of godparents. Sometimes young people come circling around me, and I bring up this language. "Do you want a godfather?" If it fits, we work out the necessary rules. "You may have this out of me, and you must not ask that." These are the old godparent laws. It's a version of the incarnation of God in Indian custom.

Sometimes Gold Is Dark

I love India, but being there can be challenging, sometimes even dreadful. During one visit, I nearly sank in the darkness.

An Indian friend and I went to Calcutta. He wanted to see his father, who lived in a politically sensitive zone near the city, where foreigners were not allowed. So I said, "Please go. I'll stay in Calcutta while you visit him." My friend tried to help me get a hotel, but there were no good ones, so I ended up in a sleazy hotel in a dark part of town. Because he was so anxious to see his father, once he got me settled, I encouraged him to go.

Within hours, a woman on the street thrust a dead baby into my hands, children with amputated limbs poked their stumps into my ribs begging for money, and lepers and corpses were lying in the streets where I walked. It was too much for me, and I didn't know how to get away from it. Normally I could just go to my room and hole up. As an introvert, that isn't difficult for me. But my room in that hotel had paper-thin walls, and someone was actually dying in the room on one side, people were screaming and fighting in the room on the other side, and there was a nightlong political rally in the square outside my window. I just couldn't take it. I had more in me than I could hold, and I started falling to pieces.

Gold comes in many varieties. Sometimes our gold is bright, but at other times it is heavy and difficult, and seems anything but golden. I had no friends and no telephone, and couldn't cope. Then I remembered the custom I'd witnessed with Krishnamurti. I needed to ask someone to be the incarnation of God for me, someone with whom I could share my burden.

I went to a park nearby to look for a candidate. After standing still and observing many people for about twenty minutes, I selected a middle-aged man who was wearing traditional Indian garb. I felt a particular respect for him. He walked with great dignity. I continued to watch him closely.

Finally, trembling, I went up to him and asked, "Sir, do you speak English?"

"Yes."

"Will you be the incarnation of God for me?" It was the second sentence I spoke to that man.

And, God bless him, he said, "Yes."

I told him who I was and how frightened and burdened I was feeling, and that I was unable to stand it. I poured out my misery, and he just listened without saying a word. Finally I wound down and apologized for splashing all over him. I felt so much better. I had my feet under me again.

I thanked him, and then I asked, "And who are you?"

He told me his name.

I said, "Yes, and who *are* you?"

He said, "I am a Roman Catholic priest."

There are very few Catholic priests in India, and I had picked one to be the incarnation of God for me. He had listened, heard, and understood. Then we bowed to each other and went our separate ways. Because he did that for me, neither of us will ever be the same again. He did exactly what I needed with a grace and a dignity that lives with me to this day.

Making the Exchange Conscious

I'm astonished by the enormity of the transfers of gold that I watch every day. It goes on everywhere. Often when I give a talk, for example, I single out someone and speak to him, putting gold in his lap. I do this to nourish myself. I used to think, What kind of adolescent impostor am I? But one day I was lecturing with Marie Louise von Franz, one of Dr. Jung's foremost disciples, and she cheerfully said, "The only way I can lecture is to find somebody I like and talk to him." What a relief! Occasionally after doing this, I tell the person, but mostly, I don't.

Generally we don't exchange gold well, and much of our depression and loneliness revolves around misunderstanding this exchange. We run around in a state of guilt. I'm a failure. This isn't working. What are they going to think about me? But when you understand the transmission of gold, you can honor it and not feel guilty. You know something indirect is taking place. You can sense it, but you can't possess it yet. Just try to remember that it's your gold that is being held by whomever or whatever. Knowing this gives you a certain dignity, which we all desperately need.

One reason we have difficulty letting people go —letting our children leave the house, letting people die—is because we have transferred our gold onto them. Wherever there is a numinous quality, there is gold. We cling to people who are the repositories of our gold and won't let them loose. If you cling to someone and cannot function when she isn't around—or let her go when she is dying—it probably means you have put gold on her. It's understandable that you regret the loss. But—difficult as it is—you can reclaim your projection and allow her to depart.

Investing in the Church

In olden times, people used to put their spiritual gold in the Church. These days, that takes place less and less. This is unfortunate; the Church would be an ideal place to put our gold. But it is difficult to make it work. I know. I've tried.

Thirty years ago, I grew tired handing my gold to people who would vanish the next day. The Catholic Church has always appealed to me. I didn't grow up Catholic and never joined the Church, but I'm of a temperament to appreciate it. So I chose a lovely Catholic church in Los Angeles, a copy of a Spanish Baroque church, a beautiful building with fine sculptures. One afternoon when no one was around, I went in and kneeled before the Virgin Mary, pouring out my gold. It was going well, and I was pleased. Then I saw that the halo above her head was a neon tube. I don't know why, but that wrecked it for me, and I haven't been back to that church since. We need to keep trying. We need to find places we can invest our spiritual gold today.

God Is Out of His Box

This may sound like a joke, but it's not. God is out of his box. In olden times, God lived in the Tabernacle on the altar of the Catholic Church, and the priest had the key. God was locked in, and the rest of us were locked out. There was safety in that. But now the box is broken, and God is loose. No one knows what to do about it.

I'd love to read a history a hundred years from now to see what we're going to do. There are wondrous possibilities, but if we don't succeed the consequences could be dreadful. God is high voltage, and if you get more than you can stand, as I did in Calcutta, you need help immediately. We can't lock God up again. We can't put him back in the Tabernacle.

In former times, the Catholic priest performed the Benediction at five o'clock on Holy Days. He would bring out the monstrance, a mandala-shaped, stemmed device with glass on both sides. The priest would put the host between the two pieces of glass and hold the monstrance by the stem using his stole, so that he wouldn't touch it directly. Then he would turn and show God to the congregation.

Those days are gone. God is not in his box or in the monstrance. He's out and firing all over the place. The eruption of alchemical gold is one of the chief signs of this. Alchemical gold can be your best, or it can be your worst.

In India, God is still in the box. In this respect, India is a beautiful, peaceful place. Everyone knows exactly what to do. There are laws for everything, and the priest still has the key to the box. If you need to know something, you consult the ancient myths or ask your guru or your father. God is penetrable, and there are answers. It's like the old Catholic world, where there was a right way to do things and a priest to tell you what it was.

It's not possible for us to go back to that. We no longer respect authority in that way. We can't get God in the box again, and it isn't clear that we can survive his being out of the box. It is like a ten-thousand-volt power surge getting into the household wiring and blowing out the circuits. These are desperate times. We have to create our own forms and our own differentiation, and we're not prepared to do it. When Jesus says, "I no longer call you servants, I call you friends," we can hardly bear it. We may be pleased for a moment, but suddenly we feel as though we weigh five tons. We can't carry all the weight, even though it is ours and always has been.

With God out of his old box, what vessel might contain him now? All psychological powers need a *temenos*, a boundary, a container. Until recent times, the container has been authority. But today we tear authority down. The tidal wave of accusations, the cry for blood, is us discrediting our own gold. We point our fingers and say it's their fault.

The only container that can conceivably hold the power of the mystery today is our own consciousness. We've pulled God out of his objective, collective containers, and swallowed him into our own psychology. Now we need the consciousness to manage this. So far, we are not succeeding.

Take Inwardly What Is Inward

All affect is interior. Any emotional impact we experience is inside us. If someone were to denounce me, spreading all the gossip and defamation he might find, I would probably wither. It would weigh me down, but the withering is my interior matter. If you hurt my feelings, it is an interior matter for me.

If you accuse me of having green hair, that won't bother me. It's not true, I'll say. But if you announce that I was rude yesterday, I'll have to duck. If it has an impact, it means there is a war inside me. You set it off, but what you set off is my business. Anything that can burn in a person should burn. Only the things that are fireproof are worth keeping. If you can hurt my feelings, they are better off hurt, because it's an error in me.

To take inwardly what is inward is a great art. I'm getting better at it. I don't get my feelings hurt as much anymore. But there are still things that make me wince. That means there are things inside me I haven't dealt with yet. One of the most powerful realizations we can have is that all affect is interior and needs to be understood and worked on in an interior way.

If someone has your gold, or even if you just think they have taken your gold, and then they displease you, you might become furious. Knowing what is going on at a deeper level can save you from that kind of suffering. You have no right to be dependent on anyone, or jealous of them. You have no right to be lonely. My saying this won't cure you in a day, but it might be the beginning of a cure. Dr. von Franz nearly knocked me over when she said, "Shyness is just arrogance." I'm the shyest person on earth! She spoiled it for me.

Reclaiming Our Projections

When we find ourselves clinging to somcone, caught in the unconscious grip and illegitimate demand on him or her, it is difficult, but possible, to let go. Dr. von Franz helped me with this when she said, "Don't behave as though your projection is a dog you can whistle home anytime you want it." The next time you ask someone to carry your gold, make the effort to know what is going on. Stay in contact with your own gold as you put it on someone else. If you ask her to carry that numinous, glow-in-the-dark quality for you, understand that doing so will obscure her from you as a person.

Naming the process helps. It's the beginning of consciousness. Why do I have such a strong feeling when I look at her? Do I really see her? Do I love her? Or am I *in love* with her, putting a bell jar of numinosity over her, which obliterates her from my sight?

We are rarely conscious of what is going on, and our gold is bouncing around everywhere, out of control. Alchemical, inner gold, our most precious possession, is sputtering on the street. We barely understand how much of what we perceive in others and the outside world are actually parts of ourselves.

Please observe the energy investments you make. The exchange of inner gold is occurring all the time. Try to be conscious of it. We cannot contain it in traditional ways. We need to create new language and new ways for increasing our awareness.

CHAPTER TWO

LONELINESS

CHAPTER TWO

Myths of Loneliness

I suffered so much from loneliness in my early life. It took me years to understand that this is a modern ailment. In places with traditional lifestyles, there seems to be little or no loneliness. In India, a friend told me, "Robert, I've never been lonely in my life. I don't know anything about it." Imagine someone who has never been lonely. Traditional people are surrounded by community, family, marriage, and religion that dictate the details of their lives. They are not vulnerable in this way. They may be poor materially, but emotionally they are more contained. Modernized Indians, on the other hand, experience many of the difficulties that we in the West do.

Only when we are not asking someone to carry our gold for us can look at him as a human being. And when we see others as human beings, it is possible not to be lonely. Others cannot assuage our loneliness. Loneliness is an interior matter. Even being in love has nothing to do with the other person. It's narcissistic. When we are in an actual relationship with another person and not just our projection, love is possible.

The collective unconscious often produces myths that tell us what is happening or about to happen in a culture. I'd like to discuss two myths about loneliness. The first is *Der Fliegende Holländer*, The Flying Dutchman. There are many variations on the story and all go something like this. A young man has committed an indiscretion, a transgression that resembles the one that caused Adam and Eve to be expelled from the Garden of Eden. He is the captain of the ship *The Flying Dutchman*. As punishment, he and his ship are banished to sail the storm clouds, where they must stay until someone loves him. He cannot ask anyone to love him. He has to wait. That's the terrible thing about loneliness. You can't ask for relief. It's a kind of paralysis. You can only hope that someone will sense your dilemma and help.

The Flying Dutchman has been banished "above" to the stormy upper world. Loneliness is always "up there," an abstraction. There are billions of people in the world. We do not need to feel lonely. But we alienate ourselves from ourselves and then we head up to the clouds, to the stormy aspect of loneliness. When our feet are on the ground, we feel connected to the energy of the world and don't feel so lonely. When we connect with the lower parts of ourselves, we are in relationship with others as well. The word *saunter* comes from the Middle Ages, when we sainted or sanctified inanimate objects, and not just people. Even the cross was sainted, and so was the earth. The earth was called Saint Terrare, and so when we saunter, we are in contact with Saint Terrare, the sainted earth. Sauntering grounds and connects us. It is an important cure for loneliness.

Every evening, as the winds whirl around the chimneys, the villagers hear the Flying Dutchman moaning, crying out in loneliness. They all rush indoors, closing their doors and windows, to keep out this awful sound. For years the young man lives like that, up in the storm clouds, moaning in the chimney tops of northern Germany.

Then, one day, a peasant maiden hears him moaning, and because of her good heart, goes out into the yard and calls to him. She asks the Flying Dutchman to come to her, and that is all it takes. He comes down and is relieved of his loneliness. They have a love affair, and his humanity is restored. Only a peasant woman in touch with the earth has the good sense to do this.

Many of us are Flying Dutchmen, and our loneliness is unendurable. We have an insatiable need for entertainment—we moderns watch TV and other screens more than seven hours a day—and for anything that might assuage our longing, especially late at night when the howling in the chimney tops is most painful. Loneliness is on the rise, and advertisers exploit this: *If you do thus and so, you'll feel better.*

There are three kinds of loneliness—loneliness for the past, loneliness for what has not yet been realized, and the profound loneliness of being close to God. The third kind is actually the solution. A good myth doesn't leave you out on a limb. It describes the difficulty, and also offers a solution.

Loneliness for the Past

The first kind of loneliness—loneliness for the past—is regressive. It attacks early in life, during adolescence or early adulthood. We want to return to the place we came from. We want the comfort and security of the good old days, the way things used to be. How many times do your dreams take you back to early times—the playground, the backyard, the tree you used to climb, your grade-school friends? This is the backward-turning loneliness, a hunger for the Garden of Eden.

There isn't much we can do about it. We can't go back. The Bible says that there is an angel with a flaming sword at the gate of Eden, forbidding reentry. Backward-turning loneliness is the mother complex, the wish to return to your mother's womb. It is especially dangerous in men, because it becomes the will to fail, the propensity to relinquish power and regress. It's the spoiler in a man, stronger than most men are able to admit. When you have an exam at school or an interview for a job and you feel terrified, this is probably the fear of success. The enemy is inside.

Loneliness for the way things used to be can spoil a marriage, wreck a job, and leave you inert in almost every aspect of life. No one is free of it. It is the wish to return to primal innocence. Grieving is another manifestation of harkening back to what was. When we lose something, sadness and loneliness are understandable, but they're backward-looking. It's not just the loss of the other. It's also the loss of an arrangement—a place to put our gold. We may not feel ready to take it back, to bear its weight, but all backward-looking qualities are doomed. We can't go backward.

The first step toward curing any psychological problem is to acknowledge it. When you can put a name and form to it, when you can say what you are lonely for, you're halfway free. Being conscious is your greatest ally. If you are able to admit to yourself how much you wish to fail, this is the beginning of a cure.

Loneliness for What Is Not Yet

As we will see in the next chapter, Dante describes the lowest level of Hell as the most difficult place of all. It is one hundred percent frozen, entirely cold. Loneliness is always cold. It's inhuman. The worst Hell is the frozen place of unrelatedness, disconnectedness. Hell ice is worse than hellfire.

The second kind of loneliness is the longing for what is possible but has not yet been realized. An alive, vigorous, functioning human being has a vivid intuition of what he is capable of. His intuition leaps forward, and he imagines what is possible. He fantasizes a perfect woman or a love affair that will touch him to the core. He feels lonely for what is not. He thinks that he sees out there what will assuage his loneliness. But that can only happen in here. When our value and sense of meaning are always outside ourselves—there is someone, something, some place, or some condition that will cure our problem, "just as soon as..."—we are stuck in an insoluble problem.

My next book should be entitled *Just As Soon As...* because "just as soon as" psychology dominates almost everyone. Just as soon as I get married, as soon as I get divorced, as soon as I have more money, as soon as the cancer treatment is over. "Just as soon as" is an intermediate stage where you sense what matters to you, but you externalize it and don't yet claim it as your own. Your felt need might be a new task, a new psychic capacity, or a new insight, but it is too soon to realize that it is your own gold. To sense this value, even if you cannot yet own it, is a start.

The first kind of loneliness—for what once was—drives us backward and downward. The second kind—for what is not yet—drives us forward and upward. At least this is a progressive loneliness. It drives us to accomplishments. But both of these kinds of loneliness *drive* us.

The Inner World Calls

There is a Hindu myth that tells us about the nature of loneliness—how it comes to be and what to do about it. It is like The Flying Dutchman, but more elaborate.

There was a fine young king. He was vigorous, strong, and a good man in every respect. He loved to hunt, and one day he was hunting deer on horseback with his courtiers. In Indian mythology, the call of the inner world, the call of the unconscious, is often portrayed as a deer that is tantalizingly close but eludes being caught.

The King and his courtiers were galloping along when the King saw a deer just out of bow-and-arrow range. He veered off and began following it, but the miraculous deer kept just outside his range. The King went plunging further and further into the forest, chasing the deer all day, so intent was he, in his masculine vigor, to catch this prized animal. By late afternoon, the King was irretrievably lost, and the deer had vanished. What a wonderful deer. He gets you where you need to go and then leaves you.

The King was exhausted and rather frightened, as he was now separated from his courtiers. Being a wise young man, he got off his horse and sat down. If you don't know what to do, sit quietly until your wits come back. Suddenly he heard a beautiful song. A maiden was singing as he had never heard before, and he fell in love with her very voice. He got up, began to walk toward the sound, and soon came upon her. The maiden was as lovely as her voice, and the King, overwhelmed by her beauty, instantly lost his heart to her.

He asked, "Are you married?" and the maiden said, "No." The King said, "Will you be my queen?" and the maiden replied, "You must ask my father." So he asked her to take him to her father, and she did.

The father, himself a wise man, was delighted at the prospect of having a king for a son-in-law, but he didn't let his enthusiasm appear too obvious. So he said, "You may have my daughter as your wife under one condition. She must never see water." If you replace the word *water* with the word *reality,* you will understand this story easily. The King agreed, and the young couple married. But there was one problem—keeping the Queen from seeing water.

Avoiding Reality

The King did his best to arrange for the Queen to see no water, but the task was more difficult than he anticipated. The palace was located right along the river that ran through the royal city. So the King ordered the royal laborers to build a brick wall alongside the river. Before he would take the Queen outdoors or up to the palace roof, he also had to be careful that there was no rain on the horizon. In fact, the King spent almost all his time arranging things so the Queen would not see water, and he did little else. The kingdom was going to seed, as he wasn't performing most of his kingly duties.

Finally, one day, the courtiers cornered him and said, "You never meet with us. You're not managing the kingdom." And the King said, "I have no time. Go away." The head courtier, seeing that the kingdom was in dire straits and that there was no use asking the King again, as he was out of his mind, went to the servants and asked, "How does the palace work? What do you do?" The servants told him, "We spend all our time making sure the Queen does not see water."

What is this myth telling us? The King is in the throes of the forward-looking possibility, but his new-found love, who would fill his heart and bring him all the legitimate happiness in the world, has a condition laid upon her—that she must never be subjected to reality. Every love affair, every stardust romance, carries this prohibition. It will work as long as you don't subject it to reality, as long as it doesn't come down to ordinary everydayness. If ordinary everydayness—water, in the symbolism of the story—ever douses this fallen-in-love quality, the feeling dissolves instantly. That is the story of romantic love.

The head courtier came to the King and said, "Sire, let us make a garden on the rooftop. We can plant trees and beautiful plants and put a roof over it, so that even if it rains, there will be no difficulty. You and the Queen can spend time in the garden and be happy." They did, and it was a success.

Contact with Reality

One day the courtier asked, "Sire, are you not thirsty for the sight of water?" And the King admitted, "I'm parched, but I don't dare pursue my wish or the Queen will be in trouble." So the courtier suggested, "Your Majesty, I can build a fountain in the middle of the garden and surround it with greenery so thick that the Queen will never see it. You can gaze upon the fountain in private and be refreshed." It was done. The King went regularly to the fountain and he was pleased.

Then, one day, inevitably, the Queen happened upon the fountain. She was delighted for an instant, and then she vanished. Our idealism, our noble motives, our loftiest intuitions perish at their first contact with reality. The Queen disappeared, and the King was consumed with loneliness. Everything he wanted in the world, and he'd had a touch of it, was gone. He could not eat or drink. Nothing could assuage his loneliness.

The courtiers tried to cheer him up. They gave him the best of everything. But when someone is in the throes of that kind of loneliness, he is inconsolable. Nothing anyone can do, no possessions, no amount of money, fame, or entertainment can break through that loneliness. We have seen something that we are not yet able to encompass, and it is snatched away. This is the cruelest loneliness of all.

The King was in the level of Hell that is frozen over, and no one knew what to do. It had never happened before, and they didn't have a cure for it. Then one wise man observed that when the Queen vanished, a small frog had appeared in the roof garden beside the fountain. He didn't know what it meant, but he had seen it. The King heard about the frog at the fountain and went up to the garden and smashed it flat with his own hands. Then he declared that all the frogs in the kingdom were to be killed. For weeks, peasants trudged toward the palace with sacks of dead frogs to collect their bounties. Thousands and thousands of frogs were killed, and the kingdom was spending all its time and energy killing frogs and carrying them to the royal palace. The King had all the frogs killed because he thought the frog was, in some way, responsible for the disappearance of his queen. That's a strange symptom of loneliness. We self-perpetuate our loneliness, killing every frog we see.

Finally, one day, the Frog King came to see the King, and he said, "Your Majesty, you are about to exterminate my entire species. I am the father of your queen. She returned to the land of the frogs when you broke your vow." The King listened. He liked the Frog King and made peace with him. As a result, the Frog King brought his daughter, the little frog by the fountain, back to life. Here was the Queen in all her splendor. The King embraced her and was happy again. And the Queen was no longer compelled to stay away from water.

Transformation and Redemption

This myth of the King and his Frog Queen is a story of transformation and redemption. If you're caught in the kind of loneliness that has no comfort and cannot be assuaged, and you can hear the wisdom of this story, it will help. This is how to get through the second kind of loneliness. If you have touched something of Heaven, something that was given to you miraculously but is not yet ready for contact with reality, when reality touches it—and inevitably it will—the dream will vanish and your loneliness will return worse than before. You must touch the inner world and learn to bear the sight of water without going to pieces. When you restore your connection to the unconscious, to spirit, your beloved will come back cured of her reality phobia.

Both the King and the Queen had learned to live without water, reality. But the King couldn't stand it, or maybe it was the Queen who couldn't stand it. No relationship can survive unless it includes reality, water. Many fine, spiritually evolved people are at the tenuous stage where they've had a sublime vision, but if any water gets on it, it vanishes. The King on his heroic journey, and all heroes, are the ones who suffer most.

At some time in every relationship, every man or woman wonders: When did my partner turn into a frog? Whether you get through this crisis hinges on your ability to see the divine. At first, we fail. The King marries the Queen, and you might hope the story will end with them living happily ever after. But they can't take it. Every marriage replays this scene, and the marriage can dissolve at this point. She turns into a frog. He turns into a boar. They are unable to sustain the heavenly vision that started it all. The frog needs water.

The bliss you experience at the beginning of your marriage is true, but you cannot stand it. If you hang on and go through the dry time—without water—the glory of your first meeting will return, less fragile this time. But you have to persist to be able to touch the bliss of Heaven *and* the trials of ordinary life.

The Nearness of God

The third kind of loneliness is the most subtle and difficult. It is the loneliness of being dangerously close to God. The proximity of God is always registered first as extreme pain. To be near it yet unable to touch the thing you want most is unendurable. A medieval proverb says, "The only cure for loneliness is aloneness."

In the Western world, loneliness has reached its peak. The old ways that used to protect us have worn thin. We're at the point where the King has killed the frog, and we feel perpetual, incurable loneliness. When we're in this kind of pain, we cry out to be freed from our suffering. But when our understanding deepens, we go off somewhere, sit still, and determine not to move until the dilemma is resolved. For some time, the journey is hellish. I don't know whether it's possible for us to get through this stage more quickly or if it is a set path we have to traverse at its own pace, not ours.

When we are able to move from solitude to vision, redemption takes place and loneliness vanishes—not because it gets filled, but because it was illusory in the first place. It could never be filled. A new kind of consciousness arises that does not find the immanence of God unendurable.

There never was anywhere to go outwardly. But there is a lot to do inwardly. The change of consciousness that turns loneliness into solitude is genius. Each time the handless maiden comes to a crisis, she goes to the forest in solitude. This is especially powerful in a woman's way. It is the feminine spirit.

Solitude and Community

As an intuitive introvert, I rarely feel lonely when I'm alone. When I was in my early twenties, I took a job in a lookout tower, fire-watching in the forest. I was alone on a mountain peak for four months, and I never felt lonely. Reality didn't catch me there. I was not in danger of my Queen leaving me. But the moment I returned to civilization, loneliness descended on me like a landslide. How could I be so happy on the mountaintop and then rubbed so raw when I came back down? I didn't want to live my whole life on a mountaintop—I'm not a hermit. I had to go back and forth, as the King did, until the visionary life could finally stand the impact of the water of reality. The Queen in me had to learn to withstand the water. It's a process. I believe that everyone who has touched the realm of spirit has had to go through this antechamber.

If you're honest and perceptive, you can tell the difference between regressive loneliness, the first kind, and the ineffable second and third types of loneliness, where you sense and then see what you cannot yet have. The second and third types of loneliness are nearly indistinguishable. If you can say exactly what you are lonely for, it will reveal a lot. Do you want to go back where you came from, to the good old days? Or have you seen a vision you can't live without? They're as different as backward and forward.

Dr. Jung said that every person who came into his consulting room was either twenty-one or forty-five, no matter their chronological age. The twenty-one-year-old is looking backward and must conquer it. The forty-five-year-old is being touched by something he cannot yet endure. These are the only two subjects of therapy.

Solitude

The Garden of Eden and the heavenly Jerusalem are the same place, depending on whether you are looking backward or forward. A person touched by loneliness is a holy person. He is caught in the development of individuation. Whether it's a development or a regression depends on what he does with it. Loneliness can destroy you, or it can fire you up for a Dante-like journey through Hell and Purgatory to find paradise. St. John of the Cross called this the Dark Night of the Soul.

The worst suffering I've ever experienced has been loneliness, the kind that feels as though it has no cure, that nothing can touch it. One day, at the midpoint in my life—a little like Dante—I got so exhausted from it that I went into my bedroom, lay face down on my bed, and said, "I'm not going to move until this is resolved." I stayed a long time, and the loneliness did ease a little. Dante fell out of Hell, shimmied down the hairy leg of the Devil, went through the center of the world, and started up the other side, which was Purgatory. I felt better, but as soon as I got up and began to do anything, my loneliness returned. I made many round trips until gradually an indescribable quality began to suffuse my life, and loneliness loosened its grip. Nothing outside changed. The change was entirely inside.

Thomas Merton wrote a beautiful treatise on solitude. He said that certain individuals are obliged to bear the solitude of God. Solitude is loneliness evolved to the next level of reality. He who is obliged to bear the solitude of God should not be asked to do anything else; it's such a difficult task. For monastics, solitude was one of the early descriptions of God. If you can transform your loneliness into solitude, you're one step away from the most precious of all experiences. This is the cure for loneliness.

CHAPTER THREE

LOVE STORY

CHAPTER THREE

The Figure of Beatrice in Dante's Divine Comedy

I want to share a love story. It is similar to a million love stories that preceded it and a million that have followed since. But this story is extraordinary because it happened to a great poet who re-corded it in the most beautiful language.

Dante was standing near the Ponte Vecchio, a bridge that crosses the Arno River in Florence. It was just before 1300, a time of great awakening in the collective unconscious of the Western world. Dante saw Beatrice standing on the bridge. He was a young man, she even younger, and that vision contained the whole of eternity for him. It was a vision of completeness.

Dante did not speak to her. He saw her very little. And then Beatrice died, carried off by plague.

Dante was stricken with the loss of his vision. She was the intermediary between his soul and Heaven itself.

Six hundred fifty years later, during World War II, the Americans were chasing the German army up the Italian "boot." The Germans were blowing up everything of aid to the progression of the American army, including the bridges across the Arno River. But no one wanted to blow up the Ponte Vecchio, because Beatrice had stood on it and Dante had written about her. So the German army made radio contact with the Americans and, in plain language, said they would leave the Ponte Vecchio intact if the Americans would promise not to use it. The promise was held. The bridge was not blown up, and not one American solider or piece of equipment went across it. We're such hard-bitten people that we need hard-bitten proof of things, and this is the most hard-bitten fact I know to present to you. The bridge was spared, in a modern, ruthless war, because Beatrice had stood upon it.

Dante went on to marry, and he and Signora Alighieri raised three children. Then, suddenly, at the midpoint of his life, he fell into a deep depression. His epic poem, *Divine Comedy,* begins by saying that he was walking along in the afternoon of his life and fell into a deep hole. No one has described the midlife crisis any better. You're going along, things pretty well in hand, and suddenly you fall into a hole.

Dante finds himself in the Underworld, and above the portal into what turns out to be Hell is a sign, "Abandon hope, all ye who enter here." Dante proceeds, and encounters Virgil, the poet from ancient Greece, Heaven-sent to guide him through the nine levels of Hell, which is a spiral downward, each level worse than the previous one. In his writing, Dante peoples Hell with his own acquaintances—even a cardinal or two—which got him into trouble. Our present idea of Hell comes in part from Dante's description. Virgil represents the intellect. The guide for the first part of your inward journey is your intellect, the masculine traits of intelligence, proportion, and good sense.

The lowest level of Hell is the worst. It is frozen. To reach the coldness of life—loneliness and meaninglessness—is the worst experience a human being goes through, worse than the fiery aspects of Hell. Under the guidance of Virgil, Dante gets to the bottom of Hell and just keeps going. You don't come out of Hell through the door you entered. You go through it and out the other side. On the other side of Hell lies Heaven.

Dante and Virgil are in the middle of the world, which is where the Devil lives. And Dante gets through that nodal point, the point of zero gravity at the center of the world, by shimmying down the hairy leg of the Devil, and finds himself in Purgatory. Hell lays out what's wrong—the hellish dimensions of life—and Purgatory begins the repair, what you need in order to be restored. You need to be treated.

The verb *to treat* comes from the Latin *tractus,* from *trahere,* "to pull or drag." The earliest therapists had a series of stones with increasingly smaller holes in them, and you were literally pulled through —the biggest one first, a smaller one next, until you couldn't be pulled through any more. You came out of this experience minus a bit of skin, but you were treated. Dante is pulled through a hole from the center of the world and begins his ascent through Purgatory, its many levels and teachings.

At this point, Virgil approaches Dante and says, "I cannot take you any further. One greater than I will be your guide from here." Dante is shaken, because he has depended entirely on Virgil. Virgil continues, "Beatrice will guide you from here," the same Beatrice who had opened the vision of Heaven for him on the Ponte Vecchio.

When one embarks on this sacred journey, one relinquishes control. This can be terrifying. You are completely dependent, a frightening prospect for a modern person. When Virgil packs up and leaves, he says, in essence, "Reason can take you no further.

From here on, it's inspiration. The vision of Heaven takes over now."

When you are ready to listen, Beatrice will appear. A man I knew who was at this point on his journey asked me where his guide was. He needed her so badly. I suggested he look for her in his active imagination. When he did, she appeared instantly and she told him, "I've been waiting for you for twenty years. You only had to ask." Beatrice will be there the moment you ask and are truly ready to listen.

Beatrice shows Dante the vision of the unitive world. She takes him through the rest of Purgatory and into Heaven. Then, at the last moment, she gives way to another guide, St. Bernard, which is puzzling. But Beatrice is the *psychopomp*—a wonderful medieval word for soul guide—who leads Dante through the deep levels of Purgatory into the vision of Heaven, a journey of wholeness and healing. Dante owes his success initially to Virgil, but primarily to Beatrice, who leads, inspires, and awakens him spiritually.

Beatrice is no less powerful a figure today. Every man has a double anima. He comes factory equipped — it is absolutely ingrained—with two visions of woman. How he manages this dilemma says a great deal about his integrity. The first is the heavenly vision, a Beatrice-like figure who leaves him speechless at the world that she opens for him. Beatrice appears early in a man's life, and all he can do is store her away until he is strong enough to reencounter her. The other vision is an earthy woman who is lots of fun, sexually attractive, and perfect for courtship. She has all the human attributes, as well as the dark aspects —a dragon, a bitch, a whore. Every man is torn between the light and dark expectations of woman. And every woman has experienced man vacillating between these visions.

The woman's animus also comes double—a knight on a white horse and a barbarian. Her soul guide, usually a male figure, will guide her in much the same manner as Beatrice guides Dante. If you're homosexual, the same thing happens, but the labels are reversed. We all follow the same path.

Beatrice, the heavenly anima figure, is the vision of all that is tender and beautiful. If you are personally unlucky, like Dante—although lucky in an impersonal way—the person who awakens Beatrice in your life will vanish or even die, separating herself from you. Beatrice can live within you only in subtle form. If you marry Beatrice, your marriage will drift off, because it is more a kind of worship than a marriage; or you will turn your Beatrice into the earthy anima image and then wonder what happened to the goddess you married. Probably, like Dante, you will marry an earthy woman who will bear children and help manage your household. You are companions, and you talk and fight and make love and go through the vicissitudes of life together. But she is not Beatrice.

At age forty-five or fifty, when you have raised your children and become accomplished in your work, suddenly you fall into a hole. The more sensitive and intelligent you are, the deeper the hole might be. A guide in the form of Virgil may come and list all the things in your life that have gone wrong. These are the nine levels of Hell. Your guide, your intelligence, will dis-illusion you. "Abandon hope, all ye who enter here" is a classical beginning to what Jung called the "individuation process," or the spiritualization of a man. If I could rewrite that sign, it would say, "Give up all expectations and presently held concepts."

The job of your intelligence is to catalog Hell for you, to tell you all the things that don't work. If your integrity is sufficient, if you go forward, Beatrice will come in the form of a radiant vision of hope and the feminine to take you the rest of the way and gently deposit you in Heaven. This will be one of the most profound experiences of your life.

Modern men and women have forgotten how to take this journey. Even with the best of motives—trying to find that vision of life that will nourish us and give meaning to the progression of our days on earth—we do crazy things. We let our marriage go to pieces and marry someone else, hoping to find the visionary feminine in her. We would do well to learn from Dante. Most important is to remember that Virgil, the one who helps us discern what is wrong, and Beatrice, the heavenly guide, are both interior figures and that this is an interior journey. It has its exterior dimension. If you are an artist, a poet, a healer, a teacher, or a mystic, you will produce outer, tangible results of your journey. But the journey is essentially inner. This is the most important thing to learn.

You will never find a Beatrice to marry, because she is in your imagination, your art, and your prayers. When you seek her in an interior way, she will come in an instant. But you must be humble enough to ask your feminine side for these rare qualities of tenderness and beauty, receptivity and love. Without doing so, it can be difficult to become truly whole. Even if you experience her as a real woman who has entered your life, the grace that has descended upon you is your inner awakening, catalyzed by this wonderful experience. It is not the other. It is in you.

CHAPTER FOUR

THE ONCE AND FUTURE KING

CHAPTER FOUR

Emergence of an Archetype

When we understand the archetypes that dominate a person or a culture, we can have profound insights into what is going on in that person or culture and even make intelligent guesses about what might unfold. In a world that is increasingly difficult to understand, it can be helpful to go back to archetypal underpinnings to see if we can gain enough of an overview to make sense of the chaos.

For me, this exploration began when I happened onto some little-known articles that Jung wrote between 1921 and 1945 about an archetype that was bubbling up in the psyche of the German people. Every German patient he saw, young and old, intelligent and unintelligent, seemed to be carrying a new archetype. He called it "the Blond Beast," because it often appeared that way in the German unconscious. By 1930 it had surfaced enough so that he was able to identify it as a reemergence of Wotan, the berserker god of wisdom and war in Germanic and Norse mythology. Wotan is, in many ways, parallel to Dionysus in Greek mythology. He's the ecstatic, attractive one—with boundless energy—who overturns so much. By the early 1930s the movement of which Wotan was the archetypal force had a name, Nazism, and it was overtaking Germany. By 1940 it was rampant, and by 1945 it had left most of Europe in wreckage.

This is a brief history of the emergence of an archetype in a culture within living memory. It isn't a good example, though, because it miscarried. But it could have gone in another direction. There had been legends throughout Europe that a third Reich would rise up in Germany and be the salvation of Europe. Jung connected the old legends with this new stirring, and for more than ten years he watched carefully to see if a new dispensation, a new kind of life, the salvation of Europe, might be emerging. But it turned out to be a stillbirth. History often sputters before it gets on the right side of a new capacity or a new evolution in human consciousness. We mustn't lose hope.

Salvation

There are legends and predictions throughout the world of the once and future king, someone who has brought about a golden age and promises to come back in the future to restore it. Arthur, the great and noble king who brought England together in the sense we know it now, is one. It is said that Arthur didn't die at the end of his reign, but was transported to the isle of Avalon, a place of healing, and that he offered, when needed, to come back. The magician Merlin, the introverted, inward-turned aspect of the Arthurian story, also said, as he was leaving, "I will come back to you again." In Mexico, just before his death, the god-king Quetzalcoatl promised to come back if he was needed.

According to Indian mythology, an avatar is sent to the earth every thousand years and at other times when there are special difficulties. Buddha was one. In India today, there are rumors that a new avatar has been born who, when he comes to maturity, will step forth to be the new savior. If we take this literally, we might be disappointed. They come and they go. But in an interior sense, it's a real possibility. A point of intersection between our time-bound world and eternity exists for us, and that's salvation. I'm fascinated by this promise of a return—the once and future king. It's a glorious promise that can give us hope.

Literalism Is Idolatry

The British philosopher Owen Barfield said something that reverberates in my mind every day. He said, "Literalism is idolatry." If you take the inner world literally into our time–space world, you lose it.

Throughout my childhood and adolescence, I was in love with the Church and devoted to it. But as I grew older, I became critical and wouldn't have anything to do with it. Later, I read a medieval text that made Christianity real for me again. It said that Christ is constantly being conceived, constantly being born in his stable, constantly confounding the elders, constantly being tried by Judas, constantly being crucified, constantly resurrecting, and, most wonderful of all, constantly in his Second Coming.

The doctrine of the Second Coming of Christ is, for Christians, the greatest telling of the story of the once and future king. Early Christians said that on the eighth day after his Resurrection, Christ will come and usher the world into the millennium, when time will end, strife and suffering will stop, and the Kingdom of Heaven will be at hand. Taken literally, this story doesn't touch me very much. It's too abstract, too far out of reach. If we wait for this literally, we'll wait till doomsday.

But when we take this story out of literalism and into the interior world, which has no time and no space, we have an immediate, living fact. If we take the full story of Christianity inwardly as a timeless fact, these possibilities are available for us to touch as soon as we are ready, or perhaps even as soon as we choose. The Second Coming of Christ is not just available to us. It is beating on our doors.

Sabbath

It was expected that Christ would return within the octave, eight days, and put an end to the cyclic nature of life. The eighth day is Sunday, and so Christians celebrate Sunday as their holy day. When we celebrate on Sunday, we celebrate the ushering into the kingdom, and we relocate ourselves outside of time and in eternity. Since it's the eighth day of the week, the expectation was that there was only going to be one of them. If we want to be logical, we could say that it didn't work, because Monday turns up. But symbolically, in the depths of our unconscious, there is only one day of the Second Coming of Christ. There is only one Mass and one day of worship. It is not a process. Christianity puts an end to process and to the cyclic nature of man's sojourn on earth.

According to Jewish custom, the Sabbath is on the seventh day. There are seven days followed by the first day again. This is the myth of eternal return. Mircea Eliade points out that more people on earth believe in the cyclical nature of time than in the linear nature of time. *Sabbath, Saturn,* and *Saturday* are all associated with the number seven. Seventh-Day Adventists celebrate the Sabbath on Saturday. Seven is the symbol of cycle.

If you deal with numbers in your dreams or in mythology, you'll get lost if you take them literally. Numbers have their own symbolism, and at this level of comprehension they are about quality, not quantity. A delightful Chinese story illustrates this. The Chinese army was in a desperate, beleaguered situation, and so the general met with his advisors to decide what to do. Should they retreat and save what they could, or make a desperate effort and try to break out? They stayed up all night discussing the pros and the cons, and at dawn they took a vote. Six said retreat, and four wanted to fight it out. So they fought, because four is so much better a number than six. This is a non-literal way of thinking. Of course they won. The story wouldn't have survived if they hadn't.

The Heavenly Jerusalem

Envision the Second Coming of Christ as an inner reality that takes place on the eighth day of the week. Eight is a symbol of infinity, as you can see when you turn the numeral eight (8) on its side. A baptismal font has eight sides to indicate that when a child is baptized, he's initiated into the eight-sided consciousness, eternity. On this symbolic level, there is nothing past the number eight. You've annihilated the cyclic nature and completed life.

A Brahman friend in India told me, "Robert, you know all about *maya*"—the Indian concept that the world is illusory, a construct. "Let me tell you about *mahamaya*." *Maha* means great. "Mahamaya is the ultimate reality. It means looking at maya with intelligence." Looking at illusion in a fresh way is the heavenly Jerusalem. This is not a promise, but a fact, right now. If you can jump out of time, which we are capable of doing, we can see any given moment as eternity. We don't have to travel anywhere or even to wait in line. This is not a new fact. It's a fresh way of looking.

As mentioned, the Second Coming of Christ is available to us as individuals when we are ready, or perhaps even when we choose. This is the Christian way of speaking about enlightenment, heightened consciousness, the experience that relocates your spiritual center of gravity. We are not bound to history. The Second Com-ing of Christ is available to us as individuals, and it will wait for us until we are able to remain steady in its presence.

This intersection of levels happens to people more than we might realize. They don't understand the structure of it, so they just walk off and leave it. But sainthood is more common than we think.

The Church and the Mass

In the medieval world there was a proverb that the Mass, the communion service, a point in which we shift from time-bound to eternal consciousness, is the interim carrier of Christ. Mass can happen only once, but it can also happen again and again. The Church was touching on a non-literal fact and teaching it in the abstruse symbolism of the Second Coming of Christ. If you have the kind of mind that can think non-literally, there are jewels like this throughout Christianity.

The Church was also said to be the interim carrier of Christ—from his resurrection until his Second Coming eight days later. It was said that Christ is like the sun, and the Church is like the moon. When the sun is farthest from the moon, the moon is full. When Christ is farthest from the Church, the Church is at its greatest power. When the sun and moon are closest together, the moon has no light at all. As the Second Coming of Christ approaches, the Church will have fulfilled its duty and can disband. There is no Church or Mass in Heaven, because they are interim carriers of the nature of Christ. Christ is present in Heaven, so interim carriers are not needed.

Many traditions posit that there are two truths: absolute and relative. In Christianity these are expressed as eternity, which is neither spatial nor temporal, and the Church, which is the human dimension. We need both—the Church as the interim carrier and the insight into a higher order of things.

Cultural Yearning

As a culture, we hunger for the Second Coming of Christ. A new kind of consciousness is stirring. People sense this. Some call it the New Age—leaving the Age of Pisces, symbolized by two fishes, and entering the Age of Aquarius, symbolized by the water bearer, a man with a jug on his shoulders pouring out water. If we take Aquarius back to his Greek roots, we get Ganymede, who was abducted from earth by Zeus and appointed his cupbearer. He poured the wine at heavenly celebrations. This means more to me than Aquarius. The one who fills the cup with wine is a predecessor of Dionysus and a forerunner of Christ, and is the ruler of the age to come, with similar expectations to the Second Coming of Christ.

The hippie movement was a somewhat naïve attempt at the Second Coming, a group of people who wanted something new, the wine of life, exhilaration, motivated by the archetype of the Second Coming of Christ. The drug culture is another manifestation—although of an extremely poor quality—of the demand for the Second Coming of Christ, for the ecstatic experience and the cessation of time-and-space-bound consciousness. When someone comes to me with a drug problem, I can often touch him by saying, "What you're doing is right. Your expectations and demands are valid. But you're doing it in the wrong way."

Discontent, chaos, and caution-to-the-wind seem to be endemic worldwide. I think it is the stirring of the Second Coming of Christ. But it needs intelligence behind it. This timeless quality needs time. We're going to blunder for a while before a new consciousness, a new grail castle, a new peak experience will find its solidity.

If the Second Coming is always available, why is the world in such a mess? The best that we are capable of can turn into the worst if we get it on the wrong level. Some of the world's worst messes, like Hitlerism, were fueled and motivated by a sublime archetypal energy. These things can misfire badly. Perhaps they need to misfire until they are mature enough for their sublime aspects to be realized.

There is great danger that the archetype of the Second Coming of Christ, or the once and future king, can erupt in a negative form again. Nazism is an example within living memory. There is nothing that human beings cannot literalize into trouble. Literalism knows no end, and literalism is the death of insight. But that sublime archetypal structure is always available in its true, interior way, for anyone who chooses to touch it and is capable of touching it. Sometimes the point of contact becomes accessible only in our deepest, darkest moments.

Balancing Heaven and Earth

St. Teresa of Ávila was consumed by ecstasy at unpredictable moments. She often found herself caught in a rapture for minutes at a time, sometimes longer. But someone observed that she was never enraptured while she was cooking her breakfast. If she were, she might burn it. Eternity can dovetail into our practical lives. It's possible for us to manage the toast and the rapture.

We need poets to rescue us from the awful contradictions we get into. Speech is literal and rational and cannot easily contain the depths of the mystery. For that we need symbols and symbolic language. During Mass—a great symbol of the intersection of time and eternity—we are liberated from space and time. But after Mass, we need to go home and cook our breakfast. We can discover within ourselves the capacity to sustain both the presence of the divine and the holiness of daily life. The two are, in fact, one.

About the Author

Robert A. Johnson was born in Portland, Oregon, in 1921. In 1933, at the age of eleven, he had a mystical experience that informed the rest of his life. After attending the University of Oregon and Stanford University, he went to Ojai, California, in 1945 to study with Indian spiritual teacher J. Krishnamurti. Two years later, he entered into Jungian analysis with Fritz Kunkel, eventually enrolling in the C. G. Jung Institute in Zürich, Switzerland. In the early 1950s he established an analytical practice in Los Angeles with Helen Luke, and after nearly a decade, closed his practice to enter a Benedictine monastery in Michigan, where he stayed for four years.

In 1967, Robert Johnson returned to California to resume his life as a therapist and to lecture at St. Paul's Church in San Diego, working closely with John Sanford. In 1974, a collection of his lectures was published by a small press in Pennsylvania, and *He: Understanding Masculine Psychology* became a bestseller after Harper & Row acquired the rights.

His gift for weaving together depth psychology, mythology, and dream work, presenting Jung's theories with simplicity and grace, continues to touch people worldwide. Robert Johnson's books have sold more than 2.5 million copies.

From 1973 to 1993, he journeyed annually to India, feeling deeply at home there. From 1981 to 2002, he frequently led workshops in the southeastern U.S. and Canada organized by Journey Into Wholeness. Today Robert Johnson lives in San Diego, enjoying the fruit of his many friendships. His life's journey is explored in depth in his memoir, *Balancing Heaven and Earth.*

Resources

www.ChironPublications.com

The bookstore at the Jung Center of Houston has an extensive collection of Robert Johnson's Journey Into Wholeness lectures on CD.
www.junghouston.org

Dr. Jerry Ruhl's website describes his collaborations with Robert Johnson.
www.jerryruhlrobertjohnson.com

Filmmaker Russ Hopkins has a website describing Robert Johnson's life and work.
www.slenderthreads.com

Please visit www.koabooks.com for more about Robert Johnson's life and work.

koa books

Koa Books publishes works on personal transformation, social issues, and native cultures.

Please visit our website for a full list of recent and forthcoming titles.

Koa Books
932 Hendersonville Road #104
Asheville, NC 28803
www.koabooks.com

Koa Books is a book imprint of Chiron Publications
www.ChironPublications.com

CHIRON PUBLICATIONS

40522746R10054

Printed in Poland
by Amazon Fulfillment
Poland Sp. z o.o., Wrocław